Summer on the Porch

Summer on the Porch

by Bern Kubiak

ISBN: 978-0-578-01547-7

For my family and friends

"Live in each season, as it passes: Breathe the air, drink the drink, taste the fruit."
Henry David Thoreau

Contents

Garden

The garden is no more;
only a reminder can be seen,
a faint rectangle foundation near a wild raspberry bush
that is boasting overgrown weeds.

Reminiscing of tilling, of work, of sweat,
I can visualize your hours and days spent here.

Dandelions run free,
yellowed armies spread throughout the emptied patch of
      silted dirt,
ready to overthrow the clover and wild onions that have
      also appeared.

Oh tomatoes.
So big.
So red.
So different from the others.

Bouncing far off the ground from their tethered vines,
a jungle within a neighborhood of brick and mortar.

You would arrive dressed in a white T-shirt;
dirt would appear around your belly,
mixed with your sweat—feeding the ground
with extra nutrients.

Muscles aged but not broken would flex against the
evening sun that warmed them in Technicolor.

Some of your happiest times were when you had
your bounty of goods that you canned and ate all year
      long.

A lone chair—you would sit and have that one beer
that seemed to call you when there was no more sun.

The months have gone by—disappearing amongst
the parcel of earth that was a canvas of green and red.

Daily sacrament of water and sun
drifts beyond our own cycle of life and death.

Where are you, gardener?
Where have you gone?

There is no harvest to talk about—
Are you one with the soil you gave so much time to?

One more tomato would suffice on a cold plate,
from you, gardener, on this August evening.

A Minor League Game

Snow on the Wasatch,
beyond the four-hundred foot fence,
that advertises oil changes and Italian sausages.

A centerfielder, in pin-stripes of mustard yellow,
dirty from the slide to home last inning,
looks like an eight-year-old waiting for his big chance,
to run, catch, or use his arm.

A huckster of peanuts, beer, and plastic bats
runs up and down the aisles sweating,
like a mad speculator in a commodities pit.

His insulated chest
looks like a marsupial mother as it bounces against his
        own chest,
running up and down the stadium steps, occasionally
        stopping
and catching quick glances of the game.

His voice roars and echoes, "cold beer here."
"Get your cold beer here." Hands raise up,
like school children wanting to answer a tough
question.

He drums out the laughter of the children next to me,
who are more interested in eating the cotton candy
and waving their plastic bats that their father bought for
        them
only minutes before the national anthem.

Ash bat splinters like a Kansas homestead during a
     tornado
from a high and tight fastball that has been clocked at
     ninety miles an hour.

Muscled hitter searches for a new stick,
as the crowd cheers him on with runners
in scoring position.

The batboy quickly picks up the pieces
of the Carolina softwood, and hands him another.

Over a quick inspection and adjustment of his crotch,
number six blesses himself for another scared turn.

The solstice of summer has begun,
as the axis of the red-stitched sphere
has moved me closer to the sun.

My hands press together in unity
with the rest of the crowd for the first time all year.

Backcountry Bob

Looking for a bit of solitude,
it found me,
with a chemist named Bob.

Aspens hold a scattering of brown leaves,
dewed pines drip moisture,
early morning smell of wood smoke from
cabins in the valley. Snow bedding on granite above me.

Mule deer blending beige
into the scrub oak that gives them cover.

I see their eyes brown with fear,
sparkling like pints of hard cider.

He speaks loudly and they disappear
into the narrow chute nearby
that offers social asylum.

I suppose I wanted to be
like those mules scampering deeper
into the woods shadowing people,
but I am not.

As I spotted Bob's walking stick
with bells attached to it,
he noticed my nervous glance and stated,
"Big bears in Glacier; that's why I bought it.
"My kids and wife actually gave it to me,
 when I went hiking on vacation a few years
 back." Only in the gift shop he told me, did he ever see
          bears.

I had to remind myself that there are not any brown
          bears
along the Wasatch. I think he read my mind
and shared my disappointment;
he wanted to have a chance with an encounter
of such romantic brutality.

He told me that his family doesn't really like the
          outdoors,
as they would rather go shopping, and this leaves him by
himself most of the time.

Bob walked and told me hiking was better
than taking his anti-depressant drugs.

He hoped to lose a few more pounds
and wanted desperately to be away from
 his windowless office.

Red-tailed hawks fly by—spirited wings of prey;
they move along with us as we go higher and higher.

Fallen trees from a past avalanche
remind me of the unpredictable forces that surround me.

Bob's heavy breathing is as alarming as his choice of
flannel, Lycra, and red-leather suspenders.

His boots shuffle and drag against the mixture
of rocks and mud that line the trail.

We stop to sit upon large boulders
that allows us a view of the valley floor,
of an inversion of yellow smog, cars,
and the cross-section of the grid.

Clouds coming in from the north change me,
winds speak of something dark.

Our conversation of ordinary life
speaks of his desperation to be known.

I decide to turn around as he continues not to make
        sense of his life.
I hear his bells faintly jingling away from me.

Bear Dream

Wet pines drip slowly
Silver-tip male sniffs downwind
Breathing beast nearby

County Donegal

Bluestacks there above silently shifting
underneath the afternoon storm that is approaching.

Peat wafts the air from barren trenches;
water runs thick with the afterthought of my continued
        steps
that are blackened with this native soil.

Grasses the color of burnt sienna wave in the distance;
crags that touch the tip of passing clouds
are swallowed up and vanish.

Knots of wind tie me up against the darkened sky
that throws continual buckets of rain at me.

The northwest—vast and sublime,
The weather is as physical as a Yeats poem,
as the satisfaction of these elemental elements brings
me no greater joy.

Flask of metal and leather fit around my hand,
as I open it to warm my insides—butterscotch and old
        leather
warm the back of my throat.

No smoke here—dried barley makes it sweet,
as the oak barrels did their job of maturation.

Ruts from tractors have made the trails I take,
and where they end, I do not find out.

The snow has arrived—sprinkled like sugar,
lying unevenly, it remains distant to my eyes.

There is nowhere to hide.
There is nowhere to sit.

Waiting for a sermon,
I have accepted this finality.

I yell out like a chieftain speaking his truths,
not wanting anything but the sky to open up
and show me who is behind this grand
experiment.

From a Seat at the Bar

*The church is near, but the road is icy. The bar is far
away, but I will walk carefully.*
                                    -A Russian proverb

Hand-drawn ale I will drink.
I find spirit, thought, and food within the structure of
        red bricked walls
and historical stories from the stained glass windows.

The altar nearby—
No preaching or sermons
of humanity's need for sacrifice and salvation.

This old church with its pews intact
brings the masses here this evening.

There is no right or wrong choice here on
what God to believe in if you choose.

I witness a miracle in the making,
as that there is too much to choose from this evening.

A chalkboard of decisions. Will it be a heavenly,
hoppy imperial pale ale; a toasted and burnt saintly
        stout;
or a pious pilsner?

I will take the Belgian Tripel. It passes beyond my lips,
and it's warm to my stomach as I conclude it's depth of
     character.

Blasting hops mingle with fruity esters—I taste
     breadfruit with
bananas mixed in with mellow hops that wait and strike
     my tongue,
when I am least expecting this assault by the elixir.

I will resist all judgment and attachment,
as forgiveness is debated about sharing this pint.

Drunken monks in the abbey chanting and drinking.
Brian buys me another pint as we agree that beer is
     within
the realms of the divine. Faith is poured in sixteen-ounce
     increments.

Prohibition had been instructed by the devil himself,
as glimmering brass tanks remain divinely inspired.

Inhibitions are diluted and conflicts ended;
as I drink another, I hope this church remains open to
     all.

A toast to church and pub.

Barn

Red barn of peeling paint and rusted nails.
Foundation of stone—early light
hits the mortar—graying touches of age.

Shapely lines of weathered wood—splintered,
offering no mistakes of perfected craft and strength.

Sun again with its magnetic shadows backlighting
ageless birch branches that give cover on the east side.

Stopping again changes nothing,
as it remains here for another year.

Corn—moving shapes and colors beseeching
yet another harvested season—life determined.

A gift at the end of the road that I pass each morning.

You Know This Young Marine

Eighteen years old.
No money for college.
Enlisted at the local mall.
Paris Island was his spring break.
Christmas in the Middle East.
An AK-47 was his best friend.
He rode shotgun in a Humvee.

Roadside bomb was layered with a distorted view of
        faith.
A fireball of metal, flesh, and lost dreams has been a
        reoccurring theme.

There was a knock at his childhood home.
Flag-draped coffin arrived in Dover.
He was written up in the local paper
as a former football star who loved to hunt and fish.

Taps played and a flag given to his mother and father..
Purple Heart will be awarded.

Semper Fidelis.

Breakfast with the Paper

Sitting at the breakfast table, cool tile numbing my feet,
the blast of heat on the nape of my neck is omnipresent.

The smell of eggs on a cast-iron skillet,
mixed with onions, peppers, and garlic, awaits me
as I unfold the rolled up paper that is wet
from being thrown on the porch without a wrapper.

Hot coffee soon greets my throat
as my mind now is open for discussion.

I glance at the morning news of this dead city
as another shooting claims the life of a young man,
mixed up with other youths who believed that turf and
          bravado
were the answers that made them men.

The strawberry jam begins to ooze
over the edge of the toasted bread
and onto my plate, then onto the floor.

Kind of like buckshot in the gut from a movie squib
that was directed by an electrical charge by special
          effects
union member.

Fake blood with a shock of reality begins to set in
as the sports page proclaims another victory for a team
from Pittsburgh.

I can't believe it since they have no payroll
and an infield that is reminiscent of an "Abbot and
        Costello" skit.

I try to save some of the red raspberry with my finger
as I always did, tempting you like a child, as you were
in so many privileged prep school ways.

The sun begins to peek and crack through the door,
blinding me temporarily while trying to read the rest of
        your letter
that is covered with crumbs and ketchup.

With my caffeine high and full stomach from breakfast,
I now fully understand that you went to become a
        Hollywood whore.

I See Them Everywhere I Go

I see them everywhere I go.
I want to hold eye contact for a few seconds, but I can't.

In dreams, on street corners, or photos that I keep.
The composition and framing are the same.

I want to make eye contact for a few seconds, but I can't.
They pause and speak softly, but I can't hear them.

In dreams, on street corners, or photos that I keep.
The days seem too short for me to stop and breath.

They pause and speak softly, but I can't hear them.
Why don't they reach out and give me their hands?

The days seem too short for me to stop and breath.
Messages that I want sent never leave my mind.
They must be curious about my life now.

It's all black and white, but I see only grey in the clouds.
In dreams, on street corners, or photos that I keep.

They must be curious about my life by now.
They can't help themselves; it's the best they could do.

In dreams, on street corners, or photos that I keep.
They can't help themselves; it's the best they could do.

The pain creeps up when a sudden thought of them
        appears.
Messages that I want to send never leave my mind.

Long walks, hot food, outdoor summer sex.
Talking little with breezy whispers.

The pain creeps up when a sudden thought of them
      appears.
I remember names, but their essence fades slowly away.

Talking little with breezy whispers.
Images of them doing simple things remain.

I remember names, but their essence fades slowly away.
I eventually tell myself that the past doesn't really
      matter

In dreams, on street corners, and the photos that we
      keep.
I see them everywhere I go.

Images of them doing simple things remain.
We eventually tell ourselves that the past doesn't really
      matter.

Why They Came

They came for the maple;
in the center of the yard you stood.

They smelled your life
as the buds began to take form.

They came for the maple;
in the center of the yard you stood.

They climbed you during the long days;
that made them strong and limber.

They came for the maple;
in the center of the yard you stood.

They saw the street get wet
as they danced under you with a song.

They came for the maple;
in the center of the yard you stood.

They watched you turn bright yellow
and put you in books with labels and wax paper.

They came for the maple;
in the center of the yard you stood.

They felt you naked in the cold
as you stood silent amidst the snow.

They came for the maple;
in the center of the yard you stood.

There is now but space,
as you were taken down by saw

They came for the maple;
in the center of the yard you stood.

The children stand on top of your stump,
looking puzzled as to what to do now.

They came for the maple;
in the center of the yard you stood.

Fireworks

Emerald green, baby blue, cherry-pie red, champagne
    white.
The sky is a sheltering hue of layered smoke, late
    evening ozone.

An artist's canvas—speckled. They hold for only a
    moment.
They smear and fall to the ball field below
and in seconds appear again in different formations.

The kids run around and roll in the front yard grass.
Natural ornaments of June bugs flicker in between
    leaves,
escaping the tiny hands that chase them.

Out of breath, they tumble below the canopy
with their collection of iridescent light show performers.

Dara is there watching them—ever the guardian of the
    young,
her magic, like the night sky, is dark and comforting.

Maire is here on the porch sitting comfortably.
She soon runs indoors when the sound of Chinese
    fireworks are in the air,
reminding her of a frightened time during a festival in
    Dublin.

I see her peaking through the iron-clad fence as she
        waits for more.
The glaze of perspiration on her porcelain skin
is highlighted by the assault from the neighbors'
        interpretations of Independence.

It is her first celebration as an American citizen.
Oh so proud of the red, white, and blue.

Drinking a lager—
I think of Jefferson who died on this date in 1824.

Writing some of the declaration in a Virginia bar,
with Adams and Franklin, fixated with grammar and
        syntax.

Dirt floors, hardwood bar, and tobacco in the air
a first draft in seventeen days.

Two hundred and thirty-two years later,
the voices of the past are needed in this country.

Who are the patriots these days?

Boom, boom, boom.

The finale of the evening program has begun
as we all realize that this is the end as we know it.

Hunky

Ninety years old and born in his mother's kitchen.
He grew up along a river that had so many bridges
of mills that made glass and steel.

They are the ones that died off
as strip malls and restaurants now stand above
those grounds he toiled over.

There were no reasons to leave this town;
it had everything, he tells me with excitement.

His family from Czechoslovakia,
arriving on the boats of hope crossing the Atlantic.

From New York to here—like a chorus line, you kept
        kicking
until you were heard and respected.

Some died as infants;
some died during their prime,
but he survived them all.

He moves slowly and in control—still a limber athlete
who tells me to find a passion and dig in.

He ate apple cores from garbage cans during the
        depression
and hauled ice from horse-drawn carriages.

Leisure wasn't invented yet for these immigrants.

He laughs and can't believe he had to endure these
      things
that made him strong and hard to know.

Sacrifice, he did—a complainer, he wasn't.

He was a hunky.
Twenty cents a day was what he took home.

Battlefield scars on his arms.
All the sweat.
All the blood.

His back allowed the city skyline to have glass windows,
as the mill had him for many years and provided his
      family
so much more.

As we flip over black-and-white photos,
he pauses as his fingers shake and memory returns,
and looks at the aged Kodak paper that comes to life.

I wonder what he is thinking as he continues to tell me
      stories,
as the flakes of snow continue to multiple just beyond
      our reach of the past.

Grand Illusions

Teton Afternoon I

An elk bugles now
I touch your thighs in the grass
Indian paintbrush coos

Teton Afternoon II

An elk bugles now
I whisper your name at dawn
Teton range in sight

Teton Afternoon III

An elk bugles now
I smell the earth in your hair
Granite shapes in the clouds

Teton Afternoon IV

An elk bugles now
I look at you with hunger
Snake River moves us to the edge

Summer on the Porch

Cemented squares pushed together,
forming a late-night stage for the two-person show.

The set dressing is a table with two chairs
with dim lights provided by the moon.

We are summer stock players,
who perform comedies and tragedies.

Green and knee-high dwarf pines surround us,
as chatty crickets play the Greek chorus.

Admittance for this way-off-Broadway performance,
are the neighbors who are willing to listen.

Conversations with my father
are like a sin that suffers no act of contrition.

Between the shades of our grey matter,
that we will smoke all evening long,
we will attest our will to make the third act
before dawn a box office success.

We understand the spectrum—of light, flesh, fluids.

I see no breaking point—the chains of the nuclei are
more powerful than I can imagine.

We have created this image,
which we both snapped in different exposures
and formats.

The darkness of the night has been brought upon us
by the clouds that have been moving as slowly as our
conversation.

The humidity is suffocating like an overprotected mother
at an amusement park who only wishes the best for her
          child.

The cocktails continue to pour themselves,
making the uncomfortable white, wicker chairs
the only place we want to be.

We know each other better than we think.
These performances of "Summer on the Porch"
will soon come to an end, and production will be no
          more.

From Outside My Living Room

The sun hits me through the window warming my left
    temple.
The cars move along going someplace.

I drink wine straight from the bottle. No bread in sight.

It's Sunday and I did go to Mass,
and gently prayed for them.

New Woman

Rules remained the same for her over the years,
as she just didn't know how to break them.

Naked bodies smell of burning sweet grass and scotch.
A born-again virgin: a new eternal acceptance.

Movements—robotic and neutral.

Lights dim as I glance at our mirrored
images that reflect primal postures of raw innocence of
flesh that unfolds itself—neither young nor old.

Summer dress—dusty boots lie on the floor
in disarray like your past—forgetting
and gaining self-knowledge for the future.

Kissing her behind her ear
sends a transmission that she recalls,
but she is hesitant until the act is repeated again.

Plasticity—her brain maps are reading my signals;
that requires little change—deep in her cortex a
sensory signal has been fired again and again.

Orbiting the room she finally comes to me
and slides her hand against the roughness of my bed
that no longer posses any threat.

Ritual with an Old Dog

A push through the door—
your tail is banging off the wall,
hot breath greets me on the edge of the bed.

It's 6:30 a.m. and you want to go for a walk.
There are days when you pant and limp,
and days when you run like you're a pup.

Sniffing.
Stopping.
I pull,
you resist.

I look at your gray chin; your black coat
is slowly leaving you as you shed more each day.
Your dark eyes always speak softly to me.

Lean legs still strong,
will run until your tongue hangs low to the ground
with your frothy saliva dribbling on your bottom jawline.

Your bite and snarl are limited only to the sounds of
        bumps
that awaken you in the night.

Give me a few minutes, I always say,
as you wait patiently at the door.

You know I must make my coffee and find that missing
        to-go cup
that I can never seem to locate.

Your lack of patience was always one of your negative
        traits,
as I broke too many ceramic mugs along the way.

You yearn to chase rabbits, eat deer shit,
and find old baseballs in the high grass.

Your bark has faint whispers of soulful songs of broken
        hearts
that only a bluesman singing will understand.
You no longer are a howler for sirens that blow in the
        night.

Your tail will always wag coming out of the woods
with those burrs attached.

You resist,
I pull.
Stopping.
Sniffing.

You know too well that I have snacks in my pocket,
as I will give them all to you at once underneath the crab
        apple tree,
where we find our shade and sense of place.

Friendship and loyalty is what you continue to give,
demanding to sit with the sun in silence.

You have lived a long life so far, my friend, with the
        fires,
burning a little slower each day.

We continue to walk that ritualistic pace that we both
        know so well.

Hometown

The murky waters remain moving
despite the youth going away.

A rusted bridge of steel—always welcoming—
is weathered from the mass exodus of the past
twenty-five years.

Silt and sand stirred
were the ingredients of a rust-belt town
that created much with clear indications of prosperity.

A slow-moving barge moves north,
bumping against the shoreline, creating small wakes
that froth and disappear.

Hauling coal from here to somewhere
has timeless color, purpose, and smell.

Molten, glowing sun, burning out against the streets,
was heaven for those who worked in the heat of the
        mills.

Hell had a zip code here—for many, it was a way of life.
Disappearing industries and good wages no more.

I can hear the pounding of tools.
I can smell the sweat of thousands.
I can taste the life that they once had.

I can see them walking home dirty and tired,
from one hill to another, after the whistle blows.

They surrendered only to their families, communities,
churches, and the clubs that they built.

Their names were difficult to pronounce,
and the foods they ate separated the neighborhoods.

They are all but gone, much like the work that they did.

Blight wasn't outsourced here;
it remains a stagnant visual that makes the past seem
        like paradise.

Empty storefronts reflect a ghost town,
without any ghosts to haunt it.

Hometown.

My Great Aunt Virginia

You sit there with your gray hair recently cut and
        washed,
in your favorite chair near the television on with volume
        on high.

Your eyes tiny globes of vision, with cataracts
limiting your simple pleasures in life.

The streetlight provides a hint of glow that
breaks through your living room curtain,
opened enough to see the children playing in the street.

Is your stare taking you back to a time
when your legs worked like those kids kicking the ball
in the air, laughing at the endlessness of this summer
        night?

There is not much to say as I just gaze at the wall of
        saints and sinners—
photos of family that bear witness to the past and
        present.

You have outlived them all, you tell me, as the night sky
is now filled with lighting strikes, chasing the children
        home.

You have been praying since you can remember—often
with rosary in hand, not knowing why the years
        continue
permitting you to remain in this existence.

You have outlived everybody in your family;
as your faith is unyielding, joining them past the tunnel
of white would be the ultimate blessing.

You have hundreds of cookbooks, but you don't cook
      anymore.
The angels in your collection have greatly protected you
      throughout
these years.

Your last romantic touch was sixty years ago, by a man
not worthy of your company.

Alone in her tidy home
I wonder who will come and see her next?

I look around at this helplessness of a long life,
and see a crucifix of Jesus hanging on the wall.

I almost want to ask a question, as to when
she will be allowed to leave.

The lights are dimmed with the television on mute,
and the June bugs flicker as I head out the door.

The Glove

It sits in the garage amongst the rest
of the Cooperstown exhibits—of wooden bats and grass-
     stained balls.

A few old cards of Spahn, Musial, and Campy
from the Dodgers remain from the spokes of your bicycle.

Your glove made by Wilson,
shaped and molded by hours in the field.

Dark brown, almost black, ripped near the thumb,
the stitching is frayed, bleeding gold thread.

Tobacco juice spit-layered in the basket
from smokeless days in the field.

I remember your stance at third base
as your body would crouch close to the clayed surface.

You would graze the tip of the earth with the pocket
          open,
just waiting for that chance to pounce for the ball.

Snuffing line drives from the hot corner,
balls skipping by like rocks in a stream
amid the puffs of white smoke of baseline lime,
you would catch them.

I believe that these gloves take on the personality
of the user.

The cow leather evolves itself into something
from a Darwinian tale that heightened your ability
during this American pastime.

After work it was catch with your sons, no matter how
          tired you were.
Rhythmic in the field—a teacher and coach
for so many in the neighborhood.

Your dreams were getting us to love the game,
and each other, and we did both and you knew it.

The glove was eventually put to rest, but when?
A white ball is hidden deep in the pocket for another
          opening day.

Near Mt. Rainer

Winding logging roads,
moss-covered trees hug it's curves.

Volcanic peak silently sits,
as fire burns slowly underneath.

A coyote runs,
bushy tail bounces off the red cedar trunk.

Damp, my bones,
thick misty vision of rock and ice
is felt but cannot be seen.

Montana 1998

Neon lights from the roadhouse tempt me.
Orange backlight from the sun against the Beartooths
brings me here.

I am drawn to the smells of grilled grass-fed cow,
college-age waitresses, and cold beer.
The solstice has begun in Red lodge, Montana.

The sign reads "dogs permitted, with owners who don't
        bite."

Cowboys, fishermen, bankers are all at the bar.
Happy hour specials with those who smell of sweet
        alfalfa,
horseshit, and old money. They are all the same when
        they cross
beneath the frame of the front door.

Mirrored reflections of the past
are resound familiarly in the present.

A wooden bear in the corner
striking a hungry pose,
with a cutthroat trout in its mouth,
frightens the children who come in
for some huckleberry ice cream.

Brother Bill and his dog, Hobbs, eventually arrive,
finishing postcards to the folks,
who he hopes will join him out here in a few years,
when he finds a job, wife, and a homestead.

Moose drool is a beer and not what you think.
Steaks and potatoes fill us as we plan our next move.

(time lapse, music begins)

Nearly ten years have passed and I find part of a poem
filled with drunken, embarrassing prose,
which found it's way back to me. Finish this, it tells me.

I change the title, the number of dry heaves, and near
          police arrest
that evening and bandage this piece of important,
          historical life transition.

Where to begin and where to end.
Montana—one of the best lovers that I have ever had.

My brother did move to Montana and found plenty of
          what he was looking for.
The dog is dead, as is my father, who visited his son
          many times over the years.
The neon lights and young women still tempt me,
and my lessons in drinking have only slightly improved.

Cardboard Joe

Joe DiMaggio's image,
in sepia tone cardstock.

Sixty years old with the corners lightly flipping up,
and a crease on his left foot.

Time in a cigar box all covered in coal dust,
hidden with letters from the past.

I found you in between other teammates
and rivals who feared you.

Dashingly thin,
pinstriped in Yankee blue and white.

A wooden bat
sitting on his shoulder—posed with a hint of
arrogance.

Before the streak
and his marriage to the blonde bombshell.

His intensity captured
and sold with a stick of bubble gum.

I think about the day some young boy
went to the corner store after school.

What to buy: soda, candy, cards, or all three?

A nickel for ten cards;
his only vice was hero worship,
reading about those heroes in box scores in the sandlot.

Too poor to catch a game,
him and his buddies listened to the radio.

The muffled static of the airwaves,
then the pitch—a sportscaster would scream
about another hit for Joltin' Joe; he rounds first
an' he slides safely into second base for another double.

I press the card close to my ear
and hear the crowds cheer and children
argue about balls and strikes.

The Pink Rose

A glimpse of life
as the bee starts his seduction.

The pink rose enjoys the attention
as it sways with petals parting.

Disappearing for seconds,
the buzzing reemerges and moves.

Shuttling yellow pollen,
commencing this early morning.

Divinity passes me again.

Seduction

Creaking bridge ends my path.

An early summer runoff along the Yellowstone
creates motion of a mountain river that is deafening.

Cold, cold, cold—the water has Arctic memories.

My body afire with salted sweat that lingers around my
          lips,
cupping droplets from a single cloud that passes by.

I thirst no more and hunger for very little.

I cross the rocky sloped maze to a welcomed game trail,
beaten from well-worn hooves and boots.

I continue over rocks with moss beards and pass charred
          pines.
Thousands of seedlings sprout and hover at their bases.

I take a nap on a soft-shouldered boulder,
as it permits me to gaze
at birds of prey and their grace of attack,
of the scuttling marmots below who are unaware that
they are just meat.

A screech owl
calls out from a distance in repetitive posturing.
Then there is silence.
Frozen movements.
A spell has been placed.

No witches,
No flying unicorns,
No gnomes to see.

Cyclical dreams of re-birth,
have brought me here once again,
awakening me only to appreciate
what reality can be utilized for.

An evening sky will soon appear,
creeping above, hinting all clear.

Contrasting colors that weave low saturation,
will create seductive forces that will not be resisted.

Winter

I never got to write you that great poem.

You were my muse since that summer afternoon,
but you woke up somebody else.

Who is this woman, and how did I end up here?

My musky residue is still on the sheets,
as it doesn't know what to do this early January
        morning,
that breaths snow, ice, and a ghost of past life.

Irrational actions are like snowflakes,
from different mothers that eventually disappear in
        time.

I feel I am trapped in a unromantic comedy at the dollar
        show.
The frames slow down as I fall silent—coffee in hand.

I decide to stoke the fire and still enjoy my morning, as
        the
silence is very rewarding.

The crackle and the embers bring me back to reality.

I realize I spent too much for this ticket
that boasted great production design,
mediocre direction, and questionable casting.

Will I be recognized by my peers later in the year
for my endless work on this dramatic feature?

I stand naked staring at the Christmas tree,
watching the dry pines begin to litter the living room
        floor below.

The icicles remain underneath, hidden by the rings of
popcorn and designer bulbs that still give me spirit.

I can now feel the heat and brittle branches
as I hope this lone angel will stay to watch over you.

The coffee is good, as usual,
but there is something different. I can taste the clove
and peppercorn. It's a seasonal thing, I tell myself.

A note sticks to the cold glass of the bungalow window
        that reads:
"Can you shovel the walk and take out the garbage
        before you leave?
"I'm heading out to reconnect with my broken dream."

The Cemetery

The granite blocks,
arranged in rows, tidy and polished.

Carved with names that read of
Poles,
Slovaks,
Hungarians.

Reservations are needed. They are all very different,
but had similar hopes and dreams.

Will they know each other now as new neighbors on the
        hill?

Voices, stories, aches, and pains of timely departures,
to lingering of years in rooms by themselves—madness.

The granite blocks,
arranged in rows, tidy and polished.

They seem unnerved by the visitors who come and
        watch.
The living are the ones that need this the most.

Medals of service, plastic flowers, a flag, a bottle of gin,
and a lone candle that burns all night, all have been
        placed
where grasses grow. Respect and remembering is what
they wanted.

Old women stand huddled close by,
and a young man wanders, kneels, and prays by himself.
They all eventually sit, talk, and hope for a response.

Some have their names already carved to show their
        commitment,
have had the arrangements made to make it easier for
        others who will
remain to come and visit.

The granite blocks,
arranged in rows, tidy and polished.

They continue to grow as silent fathers stare at dreams
        shattered.
Black dirt, no name, fresh flowers on top are repeated.

Six feet could be a friend or a lover.
A saxophone appearing in stone,
music for the parents when they arrive for the concert.

The granite blocks,
arranged in rows, tidy and polished.

The Picture Book

We are framed together in a distance,
in this leather-bound picture book.

Pacific Ocean in the distance.

I keep it in a dusty closet.
I pick it up from time to time.

I take a look at your face that stayed beside me,
along the cedars and firs.

A day to remember while
walking in between the spiraling coastal pines,
as the dampness occupied our minds.

Movements, heat, little talking,
a chess game below the canopy.

Stealing your sweet breath,
as a weak northwest sun began to shine.

I wonder about the copy of the picture,
that I sent you soon after.

Do you have it in a book?
Do you have it in a frame?
Or is it lost like a deep memory itself?

Are these book good to have, I often wonder,
as I look beyond the image, composition, and
your form.

Unfinished stories repeat—whispers
of what could have been a different beginning.

If I didn't have that book stored in the closet,
what would I have?

It's time to stop pressing against the image that
harvests this outdated matted print.

I now understand what you really needed.

The flash of a camera
created this imperfect existence.

The Road to Jackson

Gray skies of despair loom over the valleys of fertility
that roll out like canvases waiting to be used.

Sliver buildings of metal that hold potatoes
are bulging from its seams.

A recent harvest, as bodies of migrants
from the fields are plentiful, pumping gas at the only
            station
I see for miles, for the long drive back to somewhere else.

Discolored sage not having a care in the world
sits and waits for the slow death of winter to arrive.

Bales of hay still lie silent in rows,
as their sweet smell passes me by.

Miles of endless fence encompass the desolated land
that man has empowered for his own satisfaction and
        protection.

A lone bird in the sky, and I don't understand why,
circling above in a leisurely manner.

Distant mountains with snow lie ahead;
I am eager to walk amongst the granite spires and taste
        the air.
Can they have addicting implications?

To soothe my soul for a moment in time,
I notice the cottonwood trees standing still,
barely moving against the dry wind.

Low riverbeds along the Snake River,
lie partially frozen with snow, ice, and water.

An angler manages a few casts from
the bank. He continues this mastery, popping his fly
into the waters against the backdrop of the Tetons.

The rancher drives along the rutted tundra,
and he nods from his aging Ford pickup
as he passes me by taking his time.

I continue to drive through southeastern Idaho,
and the last of the fields and Mormon churches,
up toward the heavily forested pass that bears no
resemblance to where I have come from.

Quaking

High alpine yellows stir against each other,
bending their white bodies with fluidity.

Muddied trail,
I ooze into the earth.

A vacuum of high country air,
exhaling operatic sounds.

I listen and watch.

You shake and flutter,
releasing a seasonal angst.

A ritualistic chant continues
with the swirling valley mountain breeze above.

What I Got

I see her in a wheelchair. No left arm,
no left leg, no right leg. She smiles past
the stares and uncomfortable greetings.

A child on her lap hugging her. Daughter, I wonder?

She moves along with her right hand.
Directing in between the crowds,
that come to see art in July.
Her smile radiates no pain at this time,
as the hypnotic Asian drums beat against
the backdrop of a few thousand people.

Her hair, golden, moves like prairie wheat
as she dances to her own music.

People next to me in line for beer
complain about the heat, cost of gas, and clean toilets.
Do they not see and feel something of her?
Real strength isn't how much flesh you have,
but maybe the lack of it.

She soon disappears into the crowd.

Baby

Baby's breath on the tip of my nose.
Her warm heat breaks me down to surrender.

She reaches for another.
Blood and water and his muscular shoulder.

He is convinced that she will make him remain on this
    planet.
No need to fly in the evenings, as black alleys are
    forbidden.

Velvet skin with honey tones contrasts with his darker
    shades.
Father—he recognizes this important title and duties.

I watch as they dance to the music that we all listen to,
when everything in life seems to be a moment of
    perfection.

Their eyes meet and understand each other.

Seconds become minutes, and I want to freeze this
    frame, but I realize that they have already done
    so.

February

I step outside—the sun hidden between,
a lie—a transparency below the cosmos.

The groundhog silently delivers six more weeks
of winter—who is this prophet of weather?

The crunching of hard-packed snow enhances my senses
like a spider in a corner reading Bukowski by the
      fireplace.

The black crows fly overhead,
laughing arrogantly at my cabin-dweller existence.

Yard Sale

A beat-up toaster.
A beanbag chair.
A tiki torch.
A twelve-inch television.
The yard is littered with leftover plastic.

An economic afternoon slowdown is approaching.

A car stops, led by a curious grandmother.
Out comes a young girl who looks to have very little. She
        points,
and the old woman digs in her purse—rattling of change
        in her wrinkled hand,
works her way to the purveyors of this yard sale.

She buys the off-colored, stuffed white puppy dog for the
        young girl with her.

She smiles and tugs on the dog's ear.
The little girl is happy as she thanks her grandmother.

The neighbors count the money slowly and look at each
        other
as if they have just won the lottery.

April in Pennsylvania

Geometric flakes on a split-rail fence
have been driven past exhaustion.

A sense of sun returns with its warmth
on the surrounding leafy hardwoods
of cherry and maple.

Buds hesitate with this natural foolery;
deception is a common anomaly here.

A cardinal sits on the stoop—red dusting
on his feathers waiting in the sun.

Curled underbellies of organic brown mash
permit the resuscitation to begin.

Distorted paw prints take form,
as I follow a new path of backwoods
chicanery that chases the brown squirrel,
who disappears into the color of bark.

Barking dogs convince me of the omens
of springtime in Pennsylvania.

Funeral Home

Late evening of distorted
hanging faces that exhaled condolences
of their own impending mortality.

They work the crowd like desperate salesmen,
attempting to close a deal at the end of the month.

I want to go out like a Viking or Native American chief.

Crying children are frightened
by the sanitized room and the representation
of strange people who wait in line,
as if they were about to see a ghost or human oddity.

They soon realize that they anchor much needed
        support,
and stay close to their mothers and fathers and break
        small
smiles when needed.

Flowers are welcoming, as their colors and smells
seem to create a distraction for the heavy hearts.

I see people losing themselves
within the arrangements of carnations and roses.

A human life gone—
Neatly decorated with a new suit and tie.
Hair combed and skin tanned. An afterglow has
        emerged.

Hands folded neatly with rosary placed for view,
as people kneel in front—praying for his soul, or
simply talking to him as if he is still alive.

I am sure he appreciates the attention but wishes for a
        quick good-bye,
as he knows this has been too much for everyone
        involved.

I can hear him telling everyone to go and eat and drink,
and leave me alone. He would want a party.

There are chants of salvation from old men who knew
        him,
and a few heavenly prayers from the cloth who barely
        did.

Wet eyes from the family,
and white snow from the sky.

Painted covered roads will eventually
lead this party away.

Wine

I think I love you.

Please don't be put off by my aggressive behavior,
as you stand alone—not a bit interested in mingling
with the potato vodka or high-end single malts from
      Islay.

We hit it off right away.
Aisle three, past the expensive break-your-heart bottles,
those lets-be-friends bottles, and high-maintenance
      bottles.

Perhaps you're the type of bottle that I have never drunk
      before.

I see that you are on sale.
Label simple, yet refined.
You were born organically on gentle slopes of fertile
      valleys.
 You're loaded with hints of spice, cedar, and
      blackberries.

I read you with food in mind. Root vegetables and wild
      game.

I can hardly wait to taste you alone.
Please, no complexities or selfish tannins and
      overzealous sulfites
that would ruin our time together.

I hope you understand my desires with you.

The first sip.
The second drip,
just like liquid velvet running down my throat.
Where have you been all these late nights after work,
weekends, and the holidays?

We laugh and share a moment about other bottles
that never quite matched up to what we had tonight.
Why didn't I buy more of you?

The lights dim to stillness and jazz bounces around our
        outer lobes.
I want to savor you another evening, but you're almost
        gone.

To hell with rules as you stay the evening,
as we pass no judgments of past and present.

No elbow in the back or stealing my covers or
        complaining
about the most trivial things that drive me to drink.

You respect me in the morning and linger on my tongue,
but I look, and emptiness has filled the room;
suddenly your gone, and I understand.

The Deer

A corner lot in the neighborhood.

A Christmas tree in the front window gives off the color
      spectrums
against the needled fir, illuminating the living room.

A lone silhouette paces back and forth.

I can see my breath pushing in front of me toward the
      three deer,
catching them before I can get a better look.

Their necks bent in unison eating a dozen or so apples
that have been scattered on the frozen yard.

Slender bodies are in survival mode. Bodies of beige,
white tails lighter than the snow on the ground.

Seven straight nights I see them digging their noses
underneath the ice and snow, forging and hoping
for something extra.

They disappear just beyond the street lamps and
      hedgerows
when I get close.

Hunkering down like a lost battalion,
they wait until I morph into the darkened streets, as I
      have nothing to give them.

Remembrance

I woke up thinking about the horror.

The first plane was enough for me,
and had to shake the visuals from my head.

Its one of those programmed feelings
one gets when certain dates stick in your head,
no matter whether they're good or bad.

The sky is translucent baby blue—puffs of moving
white clouds that make no particular shapes are
          welcome today.

The news articles get smaller as the years go by;
as monuments are erected, widows still weep, and
families try to rebuild. Has it been this long?

Their lasting forms became ash and fire,
like with the eruption of a volcano with little time
to prepare. No place to run, no place to hide.

Evil masqueraded as men indoctrinated by others,
who preached of virgins and paradise.

"God is great."

They are the ones still burning somewhere—an endless
matchstick flickering in a dead room with no air to
          breath.

All encompassing are the emotions.
The masses spoke.
The masses listened.
The brass sang and plotted.

Bombs flew and soldiers would soon march,
in far-off places. Here we go again, America.

Bells ring on this day as I hear them in every direction.
Faceless spirits sit in parks and play chess with
        fatherless children.

Drums are still beating in Washington. How can they
        not?
Chaos amongst the chaos. Has anything changed, I
        wonder?

I pause briefly and continue to hear the names being
        mentioned,
echoing amidst the cemented walls of a city and green
        pastured farmland,
of a not-forgotten day in September.

On Being Three

He eyes my beer,
and he is only three.

He wants to dip his finger into my mug,
but I tell him no.

His eyes narrow; he tells
me that I am mean.

A transformation is happening
in front of me.

On all fours,
he postures himself,
as his flannel pajamas
take to the carpet and toys on the floor.

He turns into a bear,
and growls at everyone
who recognizes his shape-shifting abilities.

Black bear, grizzly, polar, we don't know,
as he roams the living room with grace and
dominance.

He yields to no one and bluff charges everyone
and hides behind the beanbag chair preparing his next
        move.

I keep thinking fetal position and make no eye contact,
but it's too late.

As I reach for my beer,
he reacts to my sudden movement,
and lunges for my exposed leg.

He attempts to bite me,
as his teeth grind and with a wicked smile
delivers a soft gnaw.

The saliva rests neatly below the muscle of my calf.
I look at him and he at me. Somewhere in between the
   bite,
he is slowly taking himself out of the beast.

He doesn't like what he has tasted
and runs away into the kitchen,
as he hears a afternoon snack is ready for him.

Indian Creek

Along the Colorado River I see the chocolate waters
rip and clench the rock and river edges below.

A sanctuary of new water and old rock.

The Tamarack, slender, bend back and forth,
mesmerizing me like a Vegas pole dancer.

Nudging into the cracks with red dust,
blood trickles onto the rocks with skin attached,
from the tips of my fingers.

Hanging against the sandstone outcroppings
that are shaped like tiny doorsteps that bear no welcome
        sign,
I ask for an understanding—I will make no reference
        with the word
"conquering."

Legs push me laterally toward the washed-out canvas
of an illusionary sky of muted blues and whites.

Smooth edges lie ahead,
elevating me like a released soul,
toward something unknown.

Memorial Day

I look out and see snow.
It's May—
no fancy words describing the rock face,
or the green hills that will soon enough
turn into brown earth—fire ready for the summer.

A dog barks at me and maybe
he thinks I am a poet and wants me to write about his
        day
chasing kids,
pissing on fire hydrants,
or telling me about his bitch problems.
The morning news tells of more roadside deaths
and women who want to become martyrs.

Memorial day is unfolding before me.
Flags waved, beer and meat consumed.

New white flags blowing in the wind,
placed by boy scouts, and gun salutes that made
        everyone proud.

Nomadic thoughts:
dead brothers in blue and grey at Gettysburg,
the rotting trenches of Somme,
the bloody beaches of Normandy,
the frozen fields of corpses at the 38th parallel,
the muggy, rice paddies of Southeast Asia.

Thank a vet.

The news is unsettling, and my hand is on my heart.
At least there will be new members to the V.F.W.

Bombs busting,
soldiers still dying,
civilians trying in Iraq and Afghanistan.
Policy and strategies pondered by the hawks and doves.
Who do we believe and who do we follow?

Realty shows take us away to distant locations with
        bikinis and money,
and the news is filled with overpaid pundits that spew
        hate and deception.
Purple mountains majesty—where have you gone?

Our president is in town up in the snowy mountains,
preaching the party lines of fear and loathing,
shaking dirty hands at some mogul's home,
who makes war movies for the citizenry who beg for
        more.

In Between Consciousness

You have come to me only twice
since you have left.

Nothing has been learned about your silence,
as the sun still sets in the west.

The time reads 4:44 a.m.
Too late for a nightcap,
Too early for coffee.

The crack in the window,
offers smells of fresh-cut grass.

The rain that followed—puddles
on the street look like black holes
that offer unknown answers.

On the edge of sleep,
asking the same questions;
just maybe I can think
about something else this time.

The house will soon be filled up with the
sound of passing storms that will moonlight
as answers to my never ending questions.

Past and Present

A local bar filled with un-local people,
the flash of big screens create brain maps of soft
        pudding,
dished out with barrels of booze and big hair.

Noise pollution—like a jet in the sky—falls with
        turbulent
echoing as my ear canals process disturbing splendor.

Sitting at the edge of life, drinking a sweetened soda—
eyes glued to the game, he watches, cheers, and looks
to see if he is the only one there who gives a shit.

The young and tanned bartenders throw him a seductive
        smile
while they move like crazed nymphs in a forest, pouring
        shots
of corn mash as the band starts to play.

It's been fifteen years, but I know this man. Standing
        next to him,
in ordering another drink, I think about the last time
I might have seen him.

He doesn't know me, as I notice that he has changed like
        the rest of us.
More weight, less hair, more stories to tell.

How many times have we seen people that we shared a
    moment with in the past,
but pretend and act like brown-hooded monks and do
    nothing, say nothing, and be nothing in the
    present?

I ask him if he is John—he nods skeptically,
as his oversized glasses move around the bridge of his
    nose.

He is wearing his favorite sport team sweatshirt and
    tells me
he has just come from the game.

He wants to know if I watched it here this evening.
A child-man he still is.

I have read about his brother,
who died young and left a family this past year.

My condolences are brief.

No words from him.
He points almost to the sky with his finger
and changes subjects, switching back to sports and the
    game.
He tells me that he needs to move forward like the
    games themselves.
We finally get to know the outcome and can't change a
    damn thing about it anyway.

The Lagoon

Underwater—warm like a morning bath,
No bubbles, no rubber duck to play with.

I breathe in with a heavy tank on by back,
belted weight takes me down—a plane with wings up.

Clear signs of struggle above the surface sixty years ago,
a plotted attack against the enemy in the South Pacific.

A tomb with life, coral outcroppings of color,
reef sharks on guard, currents taking them beyond the
        clarity
of the water. I see them no longer.

Below seventy feet the pressure is building;
I can feel the pressure on my organs.

A young man in a uniform
remained in the cockpit until he floated up to the top
in bits and pieces.

Quietness—a surrounding special effect echoes schools of
        fish, who are curious
and dart away when they get too close.

I look upward to the break in water.
One hundred feet—white light with dark shapes.

The taste of salt breaks into me,
as I think about the pilot's lungs filling up slowly.

Descending—not knowing how far he will go.

His last breath and my last breath—all very different.

www.ingramcontent.com/pod-product-compliance
Lightning Source LLC
Chambersburg PA
CBHW031523040426
42445CB00009B/376